" *To gulp a mouthfull of soft, warm red wine, and then to lean forward and slice a fragrant chip of meat from the brown, bubbling carcase in front of you, dunk it in the fierce sauce of vinegar, garlic, and red pepper, and then stuff it, nutsweet and juicy, into your mouth, seemed one of the most satisfying actions of my life.* "

Gerald Durrell, *The Whispering Land*, 1961

Other Books published by Maizal

Spanish
El Mate
El Tango
El Gaucho
Argentina Natural
Cocina Argentina
Vinos Argentinos

English
The Mate
The Tango
The Gaucho
Argentine Nature
Argentine Wines

Bilingual
Teatro Colón
Pintura Argentina/
Argentine Painting

www.argentrip.com

Book and Cover Design: Christian le Comte and Sophie le Comte
© Mónica G. Hoss de le Comte, 2000

Hecho el depósito que marca la ley 11.723
I.S.B.N. 987-97899-7-0
Published by Maizal
Muñiz 438, B1640FDB, Martínez
Buenos Aires, Argentina.
e-mail: lecomte@cvtci.com.ar
Printed in October 2002.
Printed by Morgan Internacional.

Mónica Hoss de le Comte

Argentine Cookery

MAIZAL
EDICIONES

Before the Spanish Conquest

When the *Adelantado* (Governor of a province under Spanish colonial rule) Don Pedro de Mendoza, arrived at the Río de la Plata in 1536 to found the City of Buenos Aires, he only met tribes of nomadic Indians who roamed the pampa collecting, hunting, fishing and cultivating some corn. The native animals were the vizcacha, the guanaco, the ñandú (the native ostrich) and the partridge and the Indians used to eat them raw. But in the Northwest of Argentina, there were Indians who had been in contact with the Inca civilisation and their habits were totally different. They knew how to cultivate the land, they had learnt how to build terraces and complex watering systems, they prepared their food in pots and the main ingredients they used were corn, potatoes, peppers and llama meat.

The Indians of the north needed a spoon to eat.

Horses, cattle and sheep brought by the Spaniards multiplied rapidly in the immense pampas.

The Indians of the central area and Patagonia quickly learnt how to tame horses, which they used in order to hunt not only ostriches but cattle and sheep as well.

These Indians used the knife to survive.

From the XVIIth century on, the main food in Argentina has been meat. "If there is no meat there is no food". Only at the beginning of the XXth century, European immigrants started cultivating fruits and vegetables in orchards near the cities.

During colonial times it had been very difficult to get manpower to cultivate the land.

Partridge, Florian Paucke S. J., (1719-1779)

Vignette on the first page of the Vera Storia by Ulrich Schmidel (1505-1579?), first historian of the Río de la Plata, (Levinus Hulsius, 1599) Schmidel rides on a llama accompanied by two Indians. The engraving symbolises the encounter of Europeans and Indians.

Gastronomic Regions

Pumpkin
Florian Paucke S. J.
(1719-1779)

Ñandú
Florian Paucke S. J.
(1719-1779)

Cover of the Chronicle "Trip to the Southern Seas" by Amédée Frézier. Allegory of Young America. Engraving by Picart le Romain, Amsterdam, (1717).

According to its different gastronomic habits, Argentina can be divided into four regions:

· The area of the Northwest has kept, more than any other area, old Spanish traditions, because this region was not influenced by immigration. Here we find algarrobos, maize, potatoes, peppers and llamas.

· The area of the Northeast has Guaraní influence. These Indians based their food on manioc and pumpkins, on fruits such as mamón or papaya, on cheese and on the exuberance of fish caught in the rivers Paraná and Uruguay.

The natives of this area had learnt the healing properties of all plants and herbs of the jungle.

· The central area is the area of partridges, ostriches, and vizcachas and after the conquest, the area of asados (barbecues). Here many immigrants settled down: the Spaniards, who brought livestock and wheat, pucheros, empanadas, jams and pastries. Later on, the English arrived, then the Germans and finally the Italians with their pasta, pizza and sauces.

· The area of the Patagonic plateau is the area of the araucaria or pehuén and the guanaco, and after the Spanish conquest, the region of horses and sheep, it is the area of the long Atlantic coast with its good tasting seafood. Here many immigrants settled down: the Germans near Bariloche produce jams of native strawberries and calafates, and established big hunting grounds; the Welsh in Gaiman are famous for their black cakes. The Jesuits who taught the natives to cultivate apples in the Valley of the Río Negro, also arrived. Trout and salmon fished in the rivers of Patagonia, together with the deer and boars caught in the area, are cooked following European recipes.

Cafés in Old Buenos Aires

*Tankard
Colonial silver*

*Tankard, Colonial
silver, XVIII th century*

*There were not many
French immigrants in
Buenos Aires and yet,
there were many
French cooks, who
influenced the Argen-
tine taste for centuries
due to their excellent
cuisine and the admi-
ration of the Argentine
people for everything
that came from France.*

Buenos Aires was founded twice, in 1536 and in 1580.
During the five years of the first foundation, a tavern
had already existed. The first inn after the second
foundation, was that of Vázquez and Vergara.

In old Buenos Aires there were many cafés, billiard
rooms and places where they served hot chocolate as
a speciality but there were very few restaurants.

People used to eat at home because they had very
good servants, the streets were neither safe nor well
lit and the sidewalks were in terrible conditions. The
native habit was to entertain friends at home and din-
ner was served early to take advantage of the light of
the sun. The most famous cafés in Buenos Aires were:
the Almacén del Rey (1769, at the Plaza de Mayo),
the Café de los Catalanes (1799), the Café de Marcos
(1801, Bolivar and Alsina), famous for the meetings
of revolutionaries and patriots, and the most famous
of them all, the Café de la Comedia of the French
Raymond (called Ramón) Aignasse. His most famous
clients were Mariano Moreno, Manuel Belgrano and
Santiago de Liniers. It was Aignasse who created
the first cookery course in Buenos Aires "for slaves
of rich houses", it was also Aignasse who offered
the catering service to General Beresford during the
45 days in which Buenos Aires was taken by the
English in 1806.

Opposite the Fortress, on the current Street 25 de
Mayo, was Juan Bonfiglio's Inn, called Los Tres Reyes
(The Three Kings). It was here that the English offi-
cers ate after the invasion: "A repast of eggs and
bacon was all they could supply, for every family uses
the purchases of the morning on the same evening,
and the markets shut very early." (A. Gillespie)

Between 1817 and 1841, the most important hotel in Buenos Aires was the Hotel de Faunch at the Plaza de Mayo. John Scriver, an English traveller who stopped at this hotel in 1825, was the first foreigner who wrote about Argentine beef, which he called "wonderful pieces of meat".

Tankard
Colonial silver

The French cook Joseph Duré together with Raymond Aignasse were responsible for the succulent banquet organised to welcome Viceroy Olaguer y Feliú in 1799.
This was the menu: Appetizers of bread soaked in ox broth covered with lard sauce of onions and garlic, roasted T bone steaks and smoked sausages; pickled partridges; boiled hens with assorted vegetables; grilled lamb cutlets; pot au feu; bouillon with boiled manioc; fruit.

Photograph by Fernando Paillet, · Basilio Marangoni's Bar, 1922

Maize

*Earthenware bowl,
Northwestern
Argentina*

*Kero, (earthenware
pitcher)*

*Emeric Essex Vidal
(1791-1861) "Plaza"*

Corn, America's gold, originated in the north of Chile and south of Peru and it was cultivated all over South America before the arrival of the conquerors. The maize plants, which originated in this area, were much lower than the plants found by Hernán Cortés in Mexico and which he introduced into Europe. There are more than 250 varieties of maize, they are classified according to their colour, size and quantity of corn in each ear; the two most common varieties are Zea Mays (sweet and tender corn) and the Everta variety, used to make popcorn. Maize, together with wheat and rice, are the most widely distributed of the world's food plants. In Argentina the sowing season is between October and November and it is harvested in January and February. Corn is the Indian wheat and the fundamental ingredient of Argentina's native food. To cultivate it, the Indians built platforms and terraces taking advantage of the slopes of the mountains, they even designed sophisticated systems of dikes for storing water.

In the Northwest there are many dishes prepared with corn: **chuchoca**, locro of fresh, roasted corn with kid meat; **chancao**, ground corn boiled in sheep fat with a lot of pepper; **mote**, corn left to cook covered with ashes, used in many stews; **tulpo**, corn flour cooked with sheep charqui (chalona) and pepper; **frangollo**, corn flour cooked in water and salt with a fried sauce of peppers and onions, similar to polenta; **sanco**, the sacred dish of the Inca, is corn with meat and tomato; **anchi**, corn

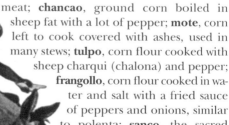

flour boiled in a broth of water, fat, onions, meat and peppers; **ancuo**, roasted corn which was eaten instead of bread. All these dishes have very few ingredients and its preparation is very slow and very simple.

"Jesus at the Pharisee's", Anonymous, Peru. The distribution of the plates on the table is an example of a rich South-American banquet in colonial times.

In the Northeast, corn is also widely used: **Paraguayan soup** is a kind of polenta; **mbaipí**, tender grated cobs with cheese and onions; **yopirá**, white corn cooked with manioc and sweet potatoes and **reviro** wheat flour boiled with milk and fat.
Some of these dishes are eaten all over Argentina: locro, tamales, humitas, carbonada and mazamorra.

In colonial times, before the end of a meal, people used to serve fresh cobs grilled or cooked in boiling, salted water. They were served with melted butter. Corn on the cob is eaten with the fingers.
Corn cut from ears of fresh corn can be served along with meat dishes and poultry. The grains can be used in mixed salads as well.

Detail of a watercolour by Adolph Methfessel (1871)

Locro

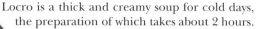

Locro is a thick and creamy soup for cold days, the preparation of which takes about 2 hours. It is made of hominy (coarsely ground maize), meat and some vegetables and it is usually accompanied by a hot fat sauce.

Before the arrival of the Spaniards, the Indians in the Northwest ate locro cooked with llama meat. The name locro derives from the aymará (aymará is a language spoken in Bolivia) word luxru. During Lent, in Santiago del Estero, a province in northern Argentina, they eat guashalocro, which is prepared using fresh grains and no meat.

Locro sauce
Ingredients
2 spoonfuls fat
4 scallions
1 tablespoonful paprika
1 tablespoonful salt
2 tablespoonfuls pepper

Braise the onions in fat and add the condiments. Mix well and continue cooking for 3 minutes. This sauce is served in a separate bowl because it can be very hot.

Ingredients
3 cups hominy soaked overnight in water
2 cups dry beans, left to soak overnight
200 gr streaky bacon cut into strips
3/4 k meat (brisket) cut into small pieces
3 red sausages cut in thick slices
4 leeks, 4 scallions, 1 kg pumpkin
1/2 kg sweet potatoes peeled and cut into pieces
2 spoonfuls paprika, 2 spoonfuls cumin seeds

Put 4 litres water in a big saucepan and add the corn and beans and leave them to boil for 25 minutes. Add the meat, bacon and sausages and cook for 45 minutes, then add the pumpkin, cut into pieces, the sweet potatoes, leeks and scallions and boil everything in low heat for 30 minutes. If it is necessary, one can add more hot water since it should have the consistency of a thick soup. Season it at the last moment. Tripe, cut into strips, can be added to the locro as well.

Humita

Humita is a soft, simple and quick meal. It is often eaten with cheese cut into pieces covering the preparation.

The secret of a good humita is the correct election of the corncobs. Choose cobs with big corn, because they contain a lot of starch which will help to form a consistent cream.

Ingredients
the corn of 10 ears of fresh corn
2 big tomatoes, peeled (remove the seeds)
1 pepper cut into small pieces
1 scallion
1 onion
2 spoonfuls fat
1 pinch of paprika
1 pinch of pepper
1 pinch of sugar
1 glass milk

Scallion

Juan León Pallière,
(1823-1887)
"Corn Grinder"

Braise the onions and the pepper in fat, but do not let them get brown, add the tomatoes and after 5 minutes, add the grated corncobs and the milk. Cook in low heat until the grain is tender. If it is too dry, add hot milk. Place the preparation in earthenware bowls, sprinkle it with sugar and heat them in the oven for some minutes so that the sugar gets brown.

Tamales

Ingredients
4 cups corn flour
2 cups boiled pumpkin
6 spoonfuls fat
1 spoonful paprika
1 scallion
3 cups empanada filling (see page 29)

Pumpkin
(Cucurbita sp)

Melt the fat and form with the corn, pumpkin, paprika and the necessary quantity of water, a compact mass and allow to cool. Take portions, hollow them, stuff them with the meat preparation and form croquettes.
Put the preparation on 2 cob leaves in cross form, and wrap the croquette as a parcel using a piece of thread or a strip of corn husk to tie them. Boil the parcels in salt water for 30 minutes.

Pumpkin
(Cucurbita sp)

Cornbread

This bread is a speciality of Catamarca, a province in the Northwest.

Ingredients
1/4 l sour milk, 50 gr melted butter
3 eggs, 3/4 kg corn flour
2 spoonfuls bicarbonate of sodium

Beat the eggs, dissolve the bicarbonate in the milk and add the eggs, butter and flour. Once the ingredients are blended, form the buns and cook them for 1/2 hour in moderate oven.

Mazamorra with Milk

Mazamorra is the rural dessert that has been adopted by the whole country.

In Buenos Aires it was sold by the emancipated slaves in the market stands at the Main Square. It is said that theirs was the best mazamorra because they carried it on horseback and the preparation was shaken thoroughly. In the Provinces of Corrientes and Misiones in the north, they call it **caguiyi**, and **api** in Santiago del Estero.

In Corrientes, mazamorra is eaten with honey which the Guaraní Indians gather in the forest. Mazamorra with honey and no milk, was eaten in the north long before the Spanish conquerors arrived.

"Birth of the Virgin"
(detail), Alto Perú,
XIXth century

Ingredients
1 l milk
1/2 kg hominy soaked overnight in 8 cups of water
200 gr sugar
1 vanilla pod

Boil the corn in water until it becomes tender, this can take some time, then allow cooling in the open air.
Boil the milk with the sugar and vanilla and add the corn; cook for 15 minutes.

Corncob
(Zea mays)

Carbonada

Carbonada is a stew or thick soup.

Ingredients
3/4 kg meat (loin) cut into cubes
70 gr fat
1 cooked pumpkin (around 5 kg)
2 onions chopped into small pieces
4 tomatoes cut into pieces (remove seeds)
1 pepper
2 cups stock
2 cups maize grains
3 potatoes cut in cubes
2 sweet potatoes cut into small cubes
2 cups of pumpkin cut into cubes
2 carrots
3 pre-cooked corncobs, cut into 3 cm rounds
salt, pepper, bayleaf, 1 spoonful thyme, some sugar.

Tomato (Lycopersicon esculentum)

Adding peaches or pears to the preparation can enhance the sweet taste of the pumpkin; in winter, dried fruits can be added as well.

Braise the chopped onions in melted fat, add the meat and lower the fire, add the tomatoes, condiments and stock. Cook for about 20 minutes and then add the cobs, potatoes, sweet potatoes, carrots, and pumpkin and cook until the meat is tender. Fruits should be added at the last minute. It has to be a juicy stew.
It can be served in a cooked, hollowed pumpkin. Cook it as follows: cut a thick slice off at the top, remove the seeds, and carefully hollow the centre, sprinkle it with water, put some pieces of butter in it, cover it with aluminium foil and cook it on a baking sheet with some water until tender.

Onion (Allium cepa)

Eduardo Pingret "Kitchen in Puebla", Mexico, 1882

Flour

The first bakery in Buenos Aires was founded in 1843 and it was called "The Cannon". Its bread and crackers were famous.

Wheat and rye were brought by the Spanish conquerors, however the Indians could also prepare bread using the flour made from the plants they found in each region.

St Katherine and the Virgin make bread for the poor, Cuzco, XVIII th century.

After the conquest, wheat bread could only be bought near the cities, where wheat was cultivated. The gaucho, the native horseman, rarely ate bread. It was impossible to get it in the country; there, only crackers could be bought, and most of the travellers agree that it was of very poor quality.

The first wheat flour was made in small domestic quern mills and bread was sold in the public square, in pulperías or it was distributed from house to house. But the Indians produced their bread using algarroba flour, manioc and corn in the North and flour ground from the pines of the araucaria in the South.

Tupo, (used by the Indians to fasten their cloaks and as a spoon), XVIII th century

Chicharrones Bread

Chicharrones are cracklings: pieces of brown tissue, left when rendering fat. This crackling bread is made in ovens on hot ashes.

Ingredients
1/2 kg flour
1/4 kg chicharrones
50 gr yeast dissolved in brine
50 gr fat

Mix all the ingredients and add the chicharrones. Cover with a dishcloth and leave in a warm place to rise. Form small loaves of bread and bake them in a hot oven until they are golden brown.

Suet Crackers

Ingredients
400 gr flour
2 teaspoonfuls salt
2 spoonfuls baking powder
100 gr suet, 2 yolks
1/4 cup cold milk

Sieve the flour, salt and baking powder onto the working surface and mix them. Form a well in the centre and add the fat, yolks and milk.
Mix everything starting from the centre and leave the pastry covered to rest for half an hour. Roll out and cut the crackers, they are usually round and not bigger than 3 cm in diameter. Prick them well; bake them on a greased baking tin in hot oven.

Araucaria

The araucaria or pehuén (Araucania araucana or imbricata) is a tree that grows very slowly in the Southern Andes over 1000 meters above sea level and which can end up being 40 meters high. Its fruit is a pinecone called "nguillú" by the mapuche Indians who harvest them in March.

Araucaria pine cone

Each pinecone has some 300 pinenuts and each tree around 25 pinecones.

*To preserve the pinecones during the winter, the Indians kept them in underground silos. When the pines were dry, they ground them to make flour which they call **chichoca**.*

When the pinenuts are tender, they eat them raw, but more often than not they are hard and they have to be boiled. It is a longish fruit and it has the taste of the nut of the sweet chestnut tree. To dehydrate them, the Indians hang them from the roof of their houses, threaded on a long string. Their children eat the crystalline resin that oozes from the lower branches of the pehuén as if it were candy.

"Among the trees that carry fruit, God created for the benefit of mankind, the Araucaria, or Pehuén as the Indians call it."

Before and after harvesting, the Indians pray around the tree. The mapuches, who live where the araucaria (also called pehuén) grows, call themselves pehuenches, "Men of the Tree".

"The mapuches worshipped the araucarias and considered them sacred trees; under their shade they prayed; they offered them meat, blood and smoke; they sprinkled them with **mushai**, the sweet, fermented chicha; they decorated them with gifts and they spoke to them as if they were people; they even confessed their sins to the trees." This is how Bertha Koessler-Ilg describes the pehuén in her anthology of Araucanian tales and legends.

Algarrobo

The algarrobo is the tree of the Argentine Northwest, it resembles the European carob tree (Ceratonia siliqua) but its fruit is totally different. It belongs to the family of the leguminosae and there are two varieties: the white algarrobo (Prosopis alba) and the black algarrobo (Prosopis nigra) which is smaller. In Guarani it is called Ibopé which means, "the tree put on the road for food". For the Indians it is the tree par excellence. The Pachamama, Mother Earth for the Indians in the north, is represented sitting under the shade of an algarrobo; there she listens to her people's requests.

The algarrobo is a 15 meter high tree with a trunk of around 1 meter in diameter. Its fruit is a long brown sheath rich in proteins, cellulose, sugar and starch. The Indians in the north prepare **patay**, **arrope** *and* **aloja** *with the fruit.*

Patay

Sánchez Labrador S. J. says: "They [the Indians] make a kind of bread from the flour of the algarroba [the fruit]; the Spaniards call it Patay [...] the preparation [of which] is very easy. They dry the algarroba beans in the sun; grind them and then sift the flour neatly. This wonderful, extra fine, clean flour is put in deep plates, bowls or in forms and is left exposed to the night dew. In the morning the flour is tight and forms a solid mass that does not break apart. People of delicate taste, mix aniseed or other aromatic seeds with the flour, before exposing it to the night dew; (bread is even more delicious with aniseed). The Indians eat this bread dry, and then they drink water; or they break it apart with a knife, put it in a glass and then they drink it", and he adds: "one can put a piece of Patay in the mouth and it is as if one would have sugar in the mouth and not flour".

Cándido López (1840-1902) "Battle of Yatay", 1865

Manioc

J. Sánchez Labrador
S. J. (1717-1798)
Natural Paraguay

J. Sánchez Labrador
S. J. (1717-1798)
Natural Paraguay

"… [Manioc] is said to have been pointed out to the Indians by the Apostle St Thomas."
Florian Paucke, P.J. (1719-1779)

Manioc (Manihot esculenta), also called cassava, grows in the forest of the Northwest and manioc flour has often replaced corn flour in those provinces.

"One can eat manioc roasted, cooked or one can prepare flour with it. Cooked or roasted, manioc tastes like chestnuts and it is an excellent food. To eat it, one has to scrape the brownish skin off."

"They replace wheat or corn bread. There are various ways of preparing flour: some wash the roots, peel them, grate them and leave them in the sun to dry. Then they grind the dry roots and sieve them using a piece of cloth; others put the roots in water where they ferment, forming a sticky foam. Then they squeeze them, and leave them to dry in the sun and then they are ground." (Sánchez Labrador S.J.). Tapioca is the starch of manioc, used to thicken soups. It is the only subproduct of manioc found on european markets.

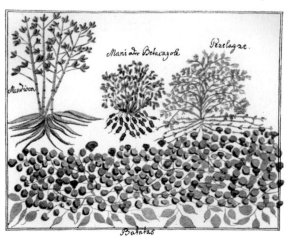

Chipá

Chipás are small loaves of bread made of manioc flour and they replace wheat bread in the provinces of Corrientes, Chaco and Misiones. Today, chipás have become very popular in Buenos Aires and they are sold in small bags in street stands all over the city.

Ingredients
150 gr fat or butter
3 eggs
150 gr grated cheese
1/2 cup lukewarm milk
1/2 lemon juice
3/4 kg manioc flour,
1 spoonful baking powder

*Manioc
(Manihot esculenta)*

Mix the lukewarm milk with lemon juice so that the milk will go off. Beat the butter or fat with the eggs and grated cheese and little by little add the manioc starch and milk until the dough separates from the bowl. Form small buns and bake them in a hot oven.

Caburé

Detail of "The Last Supper", Convent of San Francisco, Lima

Along the coast of the Paraná River, caburé is prepared with fat, cheese, brine and manioc flour. The primitive way to cook caburé is to wrap a piece of dough round a fresh branch and to rotate it on the embers until it is baked.

Empanadas

The most typical dish in Argentina, after the asado, is the glorious empanada, a must at all parties. The word empanada is often translated as turnover, but the word empanada should be used, because it has become a true Argentine creation. The original recipe came from Spain, brought by Andalusians who had been in contact with the Arabs.

The habit of putting a filling into a piece of bread or any other similar dough turns up in many cultures, but in Argentina empanadas have become a national dish.

These crisp and dripping empanadas have a characteristic recipe in each province, one can even say that each family has its own secrets which are carefully passed on from mother to daughter. Nothing is accurate when a cook mentions the ingredients of an empanada or the way in which it is prepared.

Empanadas are usually made of meat, but they can also be made of fish (tuna or cod, especially those prepared on Good Friday), chicken, ham and cheese, vegetables, shellfish, humita or filled with jam. They can be hot or cold, fried or baked.

Empanadas of the Northwest have potatoes in their filling (in Jujuy they even add peas), and in the wine region, the cooks add raisins. In La Rioja they add olives; in Tucumán they are smaller and sometimes filled with chicken and many vegetables; in Catamarca they are spicy and in Córdoba they are sweeter and larger; in San Juan they are flavoured with lots of condiments and in Mendoza they have more onion than meat. In Patagonia, empanadas are made of lamb, shrimp or hare meat, in Corrientes and Santiago del Estero they sometimes fill them with vizcacha meat. In the Northeast, wheat flour is sometimes mixed with manioc flour.

Detail of "The Last Supper", Convent of San Francisco, Lima

Luisa María
Cristofoletti De Servi
(1890-1982)
Villa Corina, Córdoba

If one prepares empa-
nadas with different
fillings, one has to
be careful and make
different scalloped ed-
ges to tell them apart.

Tips for a Perfect Empanada:

❧ *When the melted fat is added to the dough, it has to be lukewarm and one should work quickly. Do not knead the dough, just form a bun and put it in a cool place, covered by a dishtowel.*

❧ *The pre-cooked filling should be totally cold when the empanadas are filled.*

❧ *If the empanadas have to be very juicy, more onions should be added. Add the condiments when the filling is ready.*

❧ *Hard-boiled eggs and olives should be added once the fill-ing is cold, if this is not done, then they will form a purée with the filling.*

❧ *Moisten only half of the "disk" for the pastry to stick well.*

❧ *The scalloped edges should be made upwards to avoid the juice from escaping.*

❧ *Before baking, put the finished empanadas to rest, cov-ered with a dishcloth. Empanadas should be eaten right after they have been baked.*

❧ *Brush them with beaten egg just before baking.*

❧ *Put them on buttered tins, they should not stick in case the filling should ooze out.*

❧ *The oven has to be very hot.*

Platter,
Colonial Silver

Platter, Colonial silver,
XVIII th century

Empanada Criolla

Ingredients for the dough
1 kg flour
250 gr fat
1 spoonful salt dissolved in water
1 cup of cold water

Put the flour on the working surface, and pour the melted fat in the centre together with the salt, mix all ingredients into a firm dough.

Leave it to rest for an hour covered with a dish-cloth. Then, divide the dough in small portions and form small buns. Roll each bun out, the "disk" should have 12 cm in diameter and be 3 mm thick. Leave the disks to rest for 10 minutes.

This is the traditional form of stretching the dough. To simplify this step one can roll out the dough and cut it with a round pastry cutter.

Once cut, they should be allowed to rest again. Put a spoonful cold filling on each disk, moisten the edge and press firmly, the scalloped edges have to be very neat.

Put them on a table and cover them with a dishcloth.

Empanadas should be baked in a very hot oven during 10 to 12 minutes.

Serve them immediately, your guests are all waiting with a glass of red wine in their hand.

Suet (Grasa de Pella)
*Cut the pieces of fat around the kidneys in dice and put them in a saucepan until they melt. The floating cracklings (cracklings are called **chicharrones,** pieces of brown tissue left when rendering fat). Strain the fat and allow it to cool. Keep in the refrigerator.*

Empanada from the Province of Tucumán

Ingredients for the filling
1 kg loin cut into very tiny cubes
300 gr chopped scallions
600 gr chopped onions
250 gr fat or margarine
60 gr raisins
3 hard-boiled eggs
1 spoonful sweet pepper
1 spoonful spicy pepper, salt

Put the meat on a sieve and pour very hot water on it, and then pour cold water on it and leave the meat to drain. Braise the onions and the scallions in the fat, and then add the meat. When the meat is cooked, add pepper and salt; when the filling is cold, add the raisins and the hard-boiled eggs.

Pepper (Capsicum frutescens)

Sweet Empanadas

These empanadas can have different fillings: peeled grated apples with sugar, cinnamon and grape raisins soaked in rum or one can fill them with a piece of quince preserve or sweet potato preserve.
Once baked, sprinkle them with icing sugar.

In Spain the empanadas are made with oil, in Argentina oil was always replaced by fat.

F. Brambila
(1750-1832)
"Buenos Aires seen from the Cart Road",
1794

Pepper

Green pepper
(Capsicum annuum)

Pepper got to Argentina following the Inca road and at the very beginning it was only used by Indian tribes in the Northwest who prepared most of their dishes with it.

Ají or pimiento (Capsicum annuum), as pepper is called in Spanish, originated in tropical South America and it was exported to Europe in the XVIth century. Peppers can be green, yellow or red and their colour depends on the moment they are harvested and the point of maturation.

They can be eaten raw or cooked. The powdered paprika, used in the Spanish cuisine, is obtained by grinding the dried up fruits.

The guindilla pepper or chilli (Capsicum frutescens) is called Cayenne pepper. Its fruit is much smaller and when it is dried and ground, it is usually mixed in the preparation of hot sauces.

Red pepper

Pumpkin

F. Paucke S. J.
(1719-1779)
"Pepper plant"

Pumpkins fed the American Indians long before Columbus' arrival. Although there are pumpkins in Africa, India and Indochina, some varieties originated in the Andean area and in Northwest Argentina, especially the big pumpkin with yellow pulp.

In Corrientes and Misiones the native population prepares quibebe, a pumpkin purée with milk and cheese.

Quibebe

Ingredients
1 kg pumpkin, chopped into pieces
1 l water, 1/2 l milk , 50 gr fat or butter
1 tablespoonful chopped onion
1 tablespoonful chopped parsley
Grated cheese, fresh cheese

Cook the pumpkin in milk and water, drain it and make purée. Braise the onion in fat; add parsley, the purée and part of the broth in which the pumpkin was cooked. Serve with cheese.

Sage
(Salvia officinalis)

Aromatic Herbs

The mountains of Córdoba have an important production of aromatic herbs: mint, yerbabuena, carqueja, rosemary grow there. With these herbs, the famous mountain bitters are prepared.

Mint
(Mentha sp)

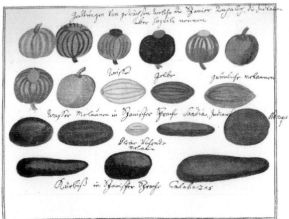

"When these pumpkins are small and look as round as small balls of bowls and their skin is very soft, the Spaniards usually cook them without even cutting them. They make a very good salad with it." (Florian Paucke)

**F. Paucke S.J.
(1719 1779)
"Pumpkins"**

Potato

Potato (Solanum tuberosum)

Potatoes (Solanum tuberosum) are tuberous plants. Apparently the plant originated in Perú, the Incas cultivated it extensively and Francisco Pizarro took it to Europe in 1534 where it was long regarded as food only fit for the poor, but the famine of 1789 made many Europeans change their mind.

Today it is one of the most widely used food plants in the world and there are innumerable dishes, which are prepared with it.

" ... a very white flour can be made from potatoes and if it is mixed with wheat flour, one can prepare excellent bread [...]. When the potatoes are taken out of the earth, one has to put them in the sun to dry, and then they have to be kept in a dark place. From these roots, a rich, thick flour which we call chuño, is made." (Sánchez Labrador S. J.)

Luisa María Cristofoletti De Servi (1890-1982) "The kitchen and the oven", Rancho (hut) of Doña Rosario L. de Pereyra, Villa Esquiú, Córdoba

In America it was cultivated in the mountains, in those places where it was impossible to grow corn because of the height.

Chuño is the starch of the dehydrated potato and the Indians knew how to store it for famine time.

In Argentina, mothers used to give their babies a drink made of chuño, milk, sugar and vanilla.

Sweet Potato

Sweet potatoes (Ipomoea batatas) also called bonia-to, camote or iñame, are a tuber belonging to the convolvulaceae family. They originated in tropical South America and the Antilles and have been eaten in America for thousands of years: 10.000 year old fossilised sweet potatoes were found in Perú.

Columbus took them to Europe on his first voyage.

In Argentina sweet potatoes are cultivated in Santiago del Estero, in Córdoba and along the shore of the Paraná River.

They taste like chestnuts and are an excellent source of potassium, phosphorus and beta-carotene.

An excellent preserve can be prepared with sweet potatoes and the only country that manufactures it, is Argentina. To prepare it, one has to peel them and make a purée. The peeled and crushed sweet potatoes are cooked and sweetened with fruit syrup and agar-agar and then flavoured with vanilla.

*Sweet Potato
(Ipomoea batatas)*

*Cultivation plat-
forms, according to
S. Debenedetti, 1818*

*Illustration by Felipe
Guamán Poma de
Ayala, 1587*

"There are two different classes [of sweet potatoes] in Paracuaria; they can have a round or elongated shape; the round ones have a red or violet skin and the elongated ones are brownish red. The red ones are as big as a fist and the biggest sweet potatoes that I have ever seen were about 15 cm long. They are white inside and have a sweet taste, sweeter than almonds. One can eat them raw but they taste much better if they are roasted underneath the ashes or if they are cooked. They are as floury as potatoes but their taste is much sweeter, as if they had been in rosewater [...] the other sweet potatoes are elongated and as thick as a liver sausage; they are also very sweet, and they are yellow inside." (Florian Paucke)

Puchero

Puchero is such a rich stew that, according to Florian Paucke, "it is a lavish storm that awakens body and soul". As so many dishes that are cooked all over Argentina, it does not have a uniform recipe, but it is cooked taking certain ingredients from each region and in each season. The first Spanish women, who arrived at the Río de la Plata, brought the recipe with them.

All the recipes have meat as the main ingredient to which a great variety of vegetables is added. In Spain it is called *cocido*, or "rotten pot"; in France, *pot-au-feu*; in Italy, *bollito*.

Leek
(Allium porrum)

Parsley
(Petroselinum sp)

Ingredients
1 kg brisket cut into big pieces
1 kg marrowbone
1 big onion cut into halves
3 carrots cut into big pieces
1 sprig parsley, 3 scallions
1 pepper cut into halves (remove the seeds)
2 leeks, 3 turnips, 1 sprig celery, 1 tomato
1 small cabbage cut into big pieces
4 peeled potatoes cut into halves
4 peeled sweet potatoes cut into halves
1/2 kg pumpkin cut into big pieces
4 corncobs 3 sausages
1 cup of rice
200 gr bacon
salt

Boil 4 litres water with salt and add the meat and the
bones. Skim and add the carrots, onion, turnips, pepper, tomato, leeks, parsley and celery, potatoes and
corn cobs, in that order.

It is Paucke again who suggests " ...do not
forget the pertinent condiment, because one
can not forget to add everything that will
incite the palate and the smell, that will
strengthen your stomach but will not dam-
age your health."

Simmer gently for approximately 1 hour, until
the meat has been tenderised.

Cook the sweet potatoes, pumpkin, cabbage, bacon
and sausages in a separate saucepan.

Prepare rice with part of the broth in a separate saucepan.
Puchero can be served with tomato sauce, vinaigrette, salsa
criolla (see page 45), salt, vinegar, mustard, etc. Puchero de
Gallina (hen stew) is made in the same way, using henmeat
instead of beef.

A Perfect Puchero

❧ Meat should be added when the water is boiling.

❧ The broth has to remain very clear, so the foam should
constantly be skimmed off.

❧ Bacon, sausages, cabbage, and all other ingredients with
strong flavour should be cooked separately.

❧ The stew should be cooked at low temperature for the
ingredients to keep their flavour.

❧ If the meat is cooked and the vegetables still need some
minutes more, then one can take the meat out and then add
it again at the last minute, so that it is served as hot as the
rest of the other ingredients.

*The stock is not serv-
ed with the puchero;
it is usually used for
a soup.*

Revuelto Gramajo

Artemio Gramajo (1838-1914), the friend and aide-de-camp of General Julio Argentino Roca (1843-1914), an Argentine President, invented a new way of eating

Cándido López (1840-1902) "Battle of Yatay", 1865

ham and eggs. This plate is famous in the Argentine and all restaurants include it in their menu.

Colonel Artemio Gramajo, (1838-1914) Cartoon by Cao

Anonymous "San Isidro Labrador", XVIIIth century
San Isidro is the Patron of the peasants who implore him to help them mitigate droughts and get good crops.

Ingredients
30 gr butter
150 gr ham or bacon cut into small stripes
1/2 kg fried potatoes
8 eggs, salt, pepper

Heat the butter and add the whisked eggs together with the bacon or ham, salt and pepper.
Stir constantly so that the eggs are cooked, but bearing in mind that the preparation has to remain moist. That is the secret. Serve the Revuelto Gramajo on toasts. Add the potatoes in the last minute.
If one wants to prepare it for breakfast, and time is short, one can use a package of ready-made potato-straws (pommes paille).

Meat

J. M. Rugendas (1802-1858) "Punta de las Vacas"

Peter Schmidtmeyer "Mule drivers in Mendoza" (1820)

Food in Argentina is based on meat, which is excellent, because it has very little fat and does not produce cholesterol.

Before the arrival of the Spaniards, the Indians ate the meat of guanacos, armadillos, ñandúes (the native ostrich), partridge and vizcacha.

The ñandú was, together with the guanaco, their basic food and they hunted them with their boleadoras. These consist of two large balls of wood or stone, covered with hide attached to two strips of equal length, to which a third strip is fastened with a smaller ball at the end of it. The boleadoras were whirled round the head and thrown at the legs of the running animal they wanted to catch.

After the conquest, the Indians in Patagonia ate ñandú meat seasoned with pepper and salt, cooked under hot stones. It was only in the XIXth century that they learnt to boil their meat together with some vegetables

Acarette de Biscay, a traveller of the XVIIIth century, says: " …there are many ostriches that roam in herds like cattle, and although their meat is good, nobody eats it, but the savages, […] their eggs are excellent and they all eat them, although they say that it has a poor digestion."

In spring and summer when the ñandúes are skinny, the Indians hunted guanacos.

In the Cueva de las Manos, Cave of the Hands, in Patagonia, there are many scenes of guanaco hunters painted on stone.

Vizcachas are eaten in stews, roasted or the filling for empanadas is prepared with it. Armadillos are roasted and their meat tastes of suckling.

Partridges, a true plague in the pampas, were also eaten on a spit. The Indians offered them to Pedro de Mendoza when he arrived to found Buenos Aires.

After the conquest, horsemeat became the Indians' favourite food.

Auguste M. Guinnard in "Three years of captivity among Patagonian Indians" (1856), says: "...most of the Pampa Indians have kitchen utensils, stolen in their pillage expeditions, and they use them to prepare their food. Women, who are in charge of this chore, carefully avoid overcooking or overroasting the food. They put water in a vessel, heat it, they cut the meat into several pieces and then they put them into the water. When meat starts getting whitish, they immediately eat it, adding some salt. They know the use of this condiment."

"Only the subdued tribes eat well done meat; yet they still prefer the lungs, liver and raw kidneys of all animals. They also drink their blood."

Patagonian Lamb
Lamb is almost the only red meat eaten in Patagonia. It is meagre thanks to the rigorous climate of the region. When the people in Patagonia prepare an asado, they know how to handle the spit: one has to bear in mind the correct distance from the fire, and the direction of the strong wind. With this meat, delicious brochettes can also be cooked.

Vizcacha

Armadillo

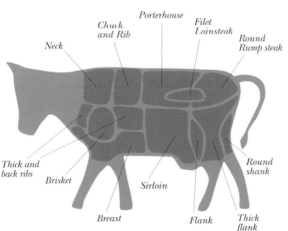

Neck
Chuck and Rib
Porterhouse
Filet Loinsteak
Round Rump steak
Thick and back ribs
Brisket
Sirloin
Round shank
Breast
Flank
Thick flank

Engravings by W. J. Holland, "To the River Plate and Back", 1913

Asado

Anonymous, 1798
"Peasant of Tucumán"

In Argentina there are three ways of roasting meat: using the grill (the most common way); the spit, where the meat is roasted perpendicular to the fire on a spit stuck into the ground; and as "asado con cuero" which is meat with its hide, preserving all its juice and essence.

On Sundays, all Argentine people prepare their asados, which are shared with family and friends. If one has a garden, there is always a parrilla, a grill; if one lives in a flat, then the grill can be in the balcony.

It is not difficult to make a good asado; a great deal of patience is necessary.

The owner of the meat, the knife and the fire is always a man. He has to take care of the asado, he has to stand in front of it for quite a long time and if somebody happens to accompany him, he will probably get a glass of wine and the first choripán, the spicy sausage in a small loaf of bread. One should never give a piece of advice to the asador, the man in charge of the barbecue.

The list of ingredients of a complete parrillada (different cuts of beef and offal served together) is very long: meat, sausages, sweetbread, kidneys, small intestines, blood sausages, etc. One can also add chicken, mutton or lamb and suckling. The asado is complete when there is abundant bread, a good salad, chimichurri (see page 44) and a good Argentine red wine. Asado and the native wine are a hard to beat combination.

The Beginning

❧ The fire should be made with quebracho (Schinopsis quebracho colorado), a tree that grows in the north, or with coal, and the grill should be placed about 10 cm over the embers.

❧ Prepare a big chopping board, and a fork and a knife with long handles.

❧ Remove the excess of fat.
The cuts of beef for a good asado should be a strip of rib, chuck, rump steak, a T-bone steak or the excellent sirloin or filet.

❧ Put the sausages in cold water for some minutes and then prick them with a fork so that the fat can flow out and the sausages do not burst.
Sausages should be roasted for 40 minutes.

❧ Put the sweetbread in water during a while so that the membrane can easily be removed. After taking it off add some lemon juice.

❧ Remove the kidney membrane and roast the kidneys in a piece at the beginning, then they should be cut into halves.

❧ One can put kidneys in salt water and leave them there for some minutes, before putting them on the grill, one has to drain them.

❧ Wash the small intestines well. Leave them in brine until putting them on the grill, roll them and hold them together with toothpicks.

❧ The blood sausages are roasted at the last minute since they are already cooked.

"There was something Homeric in this entertainment; the heroes of the Iliad and the Odyssey must have eaten their beef as we did in Entre Ríos, and I'm not surprised at their thriving upon it."
(Hinchliff)

**Juan León Pallière,
(1823-1887)
"Hut"**

**Juan León Pallière,
(1823-1887)
"La Posta, San Luis"**

A Perfect Asado

❧ The guests have to wait for the asado; the asado can not wait.

❧ The fire is made with coal or firewood; one should never use another type of fuel.

❧ Two fires have to be lit; the embers of one of them are put under the grill where the second fire smoulders.

❧ The embers should be evenly distributed.

❧ Heat the grill well before using it so as to clean it from the fat of a previous asado.

❧ A roaring fire will burn the asado on the outside without cooking it properly; a very low fire will "boil" it. The asado has to be roasted.

Silver knife (facón)
XIX th century

❧ When the juices begin to appear, turn over the meat.

❧ Salt the meat at the last moment so that the meat keeps its juice.

The facón was carried at the back of the waist in the belt; the gaucho never left his hut without it.

❧ Keep a pail of water nearby in case the fat starts burning.

❧ Cut the meat at the last moment.

❧ Each guest will eat approximately 1/2 kg meat.

❧ Start roasting the meat, then the kidneys, sweetbread, sausages, small intestines and lastly, the blood sausages.

It is better to put more embers under the meat, and use fewer under the sausages.

❧ Turn the pieces so that they are roasted evenly.

❧ Chimichurri (see page 44) and salsa criolla (see page 45) are waiting on the table.

Juan Manuel Blanes
(1830-1901)
"Balling Ostriches"
"The Lasso"

❧ The best dessert for an asado is fruit salad or quince preserve and cheese (Postre Vigilante, see page 71).

❧ Before beginning with the choripán (sausage sandwich) empanadas can be served.

Chimichurri

Chimichurri, a very hot sauce, is *the* requirement for an asado. It contains garlic, parsley, vinegar and brine.

Ingredients
10 garlic cloves, 1 spoonful dried oregano
4 bay leaves, 2 spoonfuls sweet paprika
1 spoonful thyme, 1 spoonful basil
1 spoonful chopped parsley, 1/2 spoonful cumin seeds
1 spoonful salt, 1/2 spoonful ground pepper
1/2 cup oil, 1/4 cup vinegar, 1 cup boiling water

Grind the garlic cloves and mix them with the other ingredients. Put them all in a bottle and then shake it well until all ingredients are mixed.
Chimichurri sauce has to be prepared the day before the asado and it should be kept in the fridge.

Garlic
(Allium sativum)

Charqui

Charqui is meat dried in the sun to preserve it for a long time.

The word charqui derives from the Quechua word acharqui, which means thin and dry.

To prepare charqui, meat is cut into long pieces, salted, and then left under the sun, hung from threads, for several days, so that it dries off.

If charqui is used for cooking, it has to be soaked in water overnight so that it becomes tender again.

The gaucho usually had charqui for his long voyages; he chewed it slowly. It is still used today, especially in the north.

"Around every hut on our way this day, there were short poles placed, through which strings were passed, and from them were suspended thin pieces of beef to dry in the sun, it being a favourite aliment."(Gillespie)

Salsa Criolla

Ingredients
1/4 l water, 1/2 spoonful salt
1/4 cup ground pepper, 1 l vinegar
1/2 spoonful oregano
3 bay leaves
2 peeled and finely chopped garlic cloves
1 sprig fresh rosemary
1/2 spoonful spicy red paprika
1 spoonful oil

Rosemary (Rosma-
rinus officinalis)

*Boil the water with salt. Once lukewarm, the water is mixed
with pepper and other condiments in a bowl. After 24 hours
the preparation is sieved. Keep it in a bottle in a cool place.
This sauce is served with roasted or grilled meat.*

Matambre

Red Pepper
(Capsicum annuum)

Ingredients
1 to 1 1/2 kg matambre, (flank roll)
1 grated carrot, 4 or 5 hard-boiled eggs
4 spoonfuls grated cheese, 100 gr ham
1 pepper cut into stripes, salt, pepper,
and oregano
Stock in a saucepan, to cook the roulade in it

*Put salt, pepper, oregano, cheese and the grated car-
rot on the matambre. Stretch the ham on it, the pepper
cut into stripes, and start winding the roll, beginning with
the narrow end, then add the hard-boiled eggs. Once rolled,
secure it with skewers and string and cook it in the stock on
low fire during 1 and 1/2 hours. Allow to cool in stock and
then press it. Keep it in the fridge for 24 hours. Serve cold.*

AMERICAE
PARS QVARTA.
Sive,
Insignis & Admiranda Historia de reperta
primùm Occidentali India à Christophoro
Columbo Anno M. CCCCXCII
Scripta ab Hieronymo Bezono Mediolanense,
qui istic ānis XIIII. versatus, diligēter omnia observa-
vit.
Addita ad singula ferè capita, non contemnenda scholia
in quibus agitur de earum etiam gentium idololatria.
Accessit praeterea illarum Regionum Tabula
chorographica.
Omnia elegantibus figuris in aes incisis expres-
sa à Theodoro de Bry Leodiense, sive
Francofurtensi Anno cIↃ Iↄ XCIIII Ad
Invictiss. Rudolph. n. Rom. Imperator.
Cum privilegio S. C. Maiestat.

Fish

Argentine people have always had a marked inclination for red meat; however, many Indians used to fish, especially those who lived along the banks of the big rivers such as Paraná and Uruguay.

Arco Iris Trout
(Salmo sp)

The native inhabitant of the Argentine Northeast, respectful of his environment, knows that he should only fish what he needs; if he disobeys, then the protective god of fish, would order the piranhas to attack the predator. Álvar Núñez Cabeza de Vaca (1500-1560), the discoverer of the Iguazú Waterfalls, says "when the waters are low, the Indians come to live along the riverside with their children and women, to enjoy fish... they spend a grand time dancing and singing the whole day and the whole night, knowing that they have enough to eat for a while".

Salmon
(Oncorhynchus sp)

At the time of the Spanish colonisation, in Buenos Aires, fishermen used a very curious system to catch fish: two of them entered the river on horseback holding a net from both ends. When the horse started swimming, both fishermen swam apart and began dragging the net back to the coast.

Clam
(Venus sp)

In the South Atlantic, fishing today is made, of course, from ships that leave to fish cod, brótola, sole, hake, they also fish shellfish such as **scallops** (Placopecten magellanicus) caught at the bottom of the sea or **mussels** (Musculus sp). The outer part of these mussels is of a bluish black colour and the inner part is violet, their meat is yellow. To clean them, it is necessary to scrape the outer part with a knife and to clean them again and again to wash away the sand. Then they have to be boiled in very hot water and white wine and wait until they open up. Those that do not open up should not be eaten

Scallop Shell (Placopecten magellanicus)

Theodor de Bry
"Journeys (IV)",
Girolamo Benzoni,
1594

Map of Southern America, L. Hulsius, 1603

Indian near the River Paraná, J. Edlen von Kurzbeck, 1784

Beagle Channel, C. Martens

because they are probably bad. They are served with lemon juice, light sauces and noodles or rice.

Clams (Venus sp) are of excellent taste, they have valves of a greenish colour and an elongated form.

The **squids** (Loligo sp) can be very big, and the *rabas* are the rings of the bigger squids. They are eaten either grilled or fried.

There are also crustaceans like the southern **king crab** (Maia squinado), which is very big and has the form of a spider. The Indians hunted them with harpoons, and roasted them in their canoes, where they always kindled a fire.

The southern king crab has to be boiled, it is prepared in the same way as a lobster.

Shrimps are similar to crawfish, but much smaller and in Argentina they are sold already boiled. They are eaten with lemon juice or with the famous Salsa Golf (see page 52).

Along the coast of Patagonia the Indians used to eat soups made of **algae** dried in the sun, **sea urchins**, eggs of marine birds or penguins or they prepared curanto. For the **curanto**, fish and shellfish are roasted in a hole in the earth under previously heated stones.

In the lakes and rivers near the Andes, **trout** can be fished. They are round and brown or with black and reddish spots. Their rosy meat has an excellent taste. Three varieties of trout are found in Southern Argentina: "the rainbow trout", "the brown trout" and the "salmon like trout". The most popular dish is called "trout in black butter".

Salmon that thrive in the lakes in the south, were sowed in 1904 with spawns coming from the United States. They are prepared by cooking them in water and white wine for 20 minutes. Water should not boil, leave it to simmer and serve with a butter sauce, lemon juice and white wine.

Legend of the Dorado

For the matacos, Indians of Northeast Argentina, at the beginning of time, fish lived inside a yuchán, (Chorisia speciosa) a tree which is also called the Drunken Tree (Palo Borracho) because its trunk has the form of a bottle.

Chilaj, the god in charge of fish, granted the Indians permission to fish freely but he forbade them to fish for the Dorado (Salminus maxilocua), (dorado means golden), the dorado was the forbidden fruit. But, as it always happens, there was one who disobeyed: it was Tokjwaj, he stole a succulent Dorado. In consequence of this bad action, the tree burst and the pieces of the Yuchán formed the rivers Pilcomayo and Bermejo.

Members of Cavendish's expedition in Puerto Deseado, 1784

R. Argelés, (1894-1979) "Fishermen"

Dorado

The dorado (Salminus maxillosus) is a large river fish caught in summer. Its body is round and compact and it has quite a big head. Its back is blackish blue and the sides are silver. Fishermen call it the "Tiger of the Paraná" for its fighting spirit. Its meat is excellent yet it is very bony, and the best way to prepare it, is to roast it gently on a grill, so that it looses its fat. In Corrientes they eat it stuffed with onions, oregano, breadcrumbs, parsley and tomatoes. Before putting it on the grill, oil is spread on it and then it is sprinkled with breadcrumbs and chopped bay leaves. Juana Manuela Gorriti (1818-1892), who wrote a famous cook book says: "Its meat is extremely white and so exquisite that if the riverside girls, when, taking a bath, fish a dorado in their nets, they let the other prisoners escape, thankful because of the valuable catch."

*Dorado
(Salminus maxillosus)*

Palometa

The Palometa (Serrasalmus aureus) is a river fish and one can catch it the whole year round. It has sharp teeth (one has to be very careful with the palometa because it bites), it has an oval form, the body is flat, the back is blue and it has a bluish white stomach. Its rosy meat is greasy; and has not many bones. Florian Paucke compares its form with an iron: "short and wide".

*Palometa
(Serrasalmus aureus)*

The best form to prepare it, is on the grill, but it can also be served cooked in the oven or boiled in a stew.

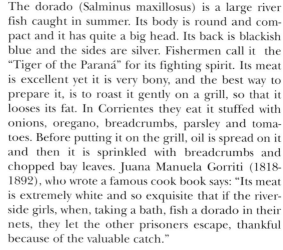

Pejerrey

The silver coloured pejerrey (Basilichthys bonariensis) which can be caught the whole year round, lives in the rivers in the north and one can catch it in the sea and in some lagoons as well. Its meat is white and it has an excellent taste. It has a blueish silver colour with darker bands on the sides. Pejerrey can be prepared in different ways: as filets with lemon juice, stuffed, boiled or baked in the oven. It appears as Gran Paraná in the menu of all restaurants.

Pejerrey (Basilichthys bonariensis)

The Gran Paraná is poached in the oven during twenty minutes and served in its sauce with cream, potatoes cut into slices, lemon and fresh parsley. It is usually eaten with rice.

Surubí

Surubí (Pseudoplatystoma fasciatum or coruscans)

The surubí (Pseudoplatystoma fasciatum or coruscans) is a river fish and it can be caught the whole year round. Its round body has no flakes, and its ashen coloured skin has some dark stains, its meat is yellowish and soft and tastes wonderful. One can roast it on the grill or in the oven and it is usually served with tomato sauce.

E. E. Vidal (1791-1861) "Fishermen"

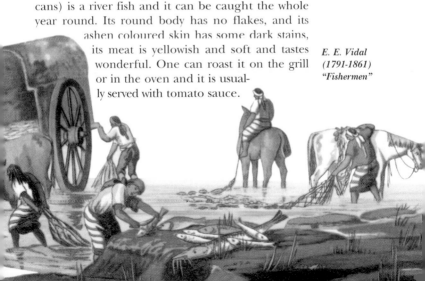

King Crab Salad

Ingredients
1/2 kg king crab cut into fine slices
1 chopped blanched onion
3 spoonfuls oil
1 spoonful vinegar; salt and pepper

Mix all ingredients and allow them to macerate.

Southern King Crab
(Maia squinado)

Golf Sauce

"He, who has invented a new dish, has done more
for mankind, than the one who has discovered a new star."
Brillat Savarin

Avocado with Golf Sauce
This is the best way to prepare avocado: cut it in half and fill it with shrimps, lemon juice, a pinch of salt and abundant salsa golf.

The tomato-ketchup and mayonnaise mixture was the inspiration of an Argentine Nobel Prize winner, Doctor Luis Federico Leloir. When he was in his twenties, and still a medicine student, Doctor Leloir used to eat shellfish in the Golf Club in Mar del Plata. Tired of eating it with mayonnaise, he asked the waiter to bring all condiments he had at hand. After tasting several combinations, the best mixture was that of mayonnaise and tomato-ketchup. As this happened in the Golf Club, Doctor Leloir called the sauce Golf Sauce, Salsa Golf.

His friends say that Doctor Leloir later complained for not having patented his idea, because with the rights of the formula he would have paid many investigators and scholarships. In Argentina almost everything is eaten with Golf Sauce.

Anonymous, "Archangel St Raphael", Cuzco, XVIII century

Alcoholic Drinks

Zoomorphic earthen-ware vessel with "bridge handle"

These vessels and bottles that represent animals were made by the Indians of the Northwest (Andean area).

In America, the process of fermentation was known long before the arrival of the Spaniards. The Indians prepared Chicha, Aloja, Guarapo, Chavü and many other drinks using the fruits of each region and fermenting them in different ways.

Chicha is a highly alcoholic drink obtained from the fermentation of cornmeal. The Indians in the Northwest prepared it with grains of maize and sugar dissolved in water or in human saliva. Indian women chewed corn and then spat it into an earthenware bowl where it was left to ferment together with some pieces of meat. Needless to say that this way of preparing chicha is forbidden.

Juana Manuela Gorriti says about the chicha: "Chicha feeds the Indians in the north, chicha is also a cooling drink on a hot day and with chicha they sometimes get drunk, to forget their miseries."

For Carnival the impassive faces of the Indians look happy. The source of their happiness is chicha. Today it is prepared with molasses and is then distilled.

Caraguatá liquor, which is made in the provinces of the Northeast, is prepared with the fruit of a wild plant which resembles a small pineapple. The caraguatá is peeled and cut into small pieces, which are left in caña (sugar cane spirit), for a whole month. After straining it, syrup is added.

This liquor is, blended with honey, an excellent cough medicine.

Aloja is the Indian beer and it is drunk in all popular celebrations of the Argentine Northwest. The first alojas are drunk for Christmas and the last ones for Carnival. To make aloja one has to grind the fruit of the Algarrobo Blanco (Prosopis alba) in a mortar

and mix it with cold water. It is a fresh and
pleasant drink, which has digestive and
diuretic properties. It can also
be made of Molle (Schinus arei-
ra) or corn.

The refreshing **Ullpada** is prepared
with corn flour and is drunk by the
shepherds in the Provinces of Salta
and Jujuy.

*M. Pérez Holguín
"Ecstasy of San
Pedro de Alcántara"
XVIII th century*

Caña, sugar cane spirit, is sometimes drunk with honey, whisking three parts of cane with one of honey.
The Mapuche Indians who lived in northern Patagonia prepared a great variety of alcoholic drinks but
they never drank them during their meals. Drinking
was for them a special rite and once they had begun,
they drank until nothing was left over. Lucio V.
Mansilla (1831-1913) in his "Trip to the Ranqueles"
says: "They [the Indians] don't drink while they eat.
Drinking is something separate and nothing gives
them more pleasure. Everything is postponed if
there is something to drink. And, as a warrior prepares his weapons for a battle, so they hide their
weapons when they prepare to drink. While they
have something to drink, they drink; they drink for
an hour, for a day, for two days, for two months. They
can spend their time drinking until they burst. To
drink is to forget, to laugh, to enjoy."

*The **guarapo** is a
beverage prepared
with sugar cane or
honey and hot water.
There was always a
jar full of guarapo in
the fields for the peas-
ants to drink.*

When, after a malón, (an Indian raid), they got **huin-
capülku** (the liquor of the Christians, pülku is the
generic name for drink), they got drunk with huin-
capülku, if not, they drunk the drinks prepared by
themselves, since they did not know the distillation
process they prepared them by simple fermentation.
They prepared **chavü** using the pine nuts of the
araucaria or pehuén (Araucaria araucana or imbricata). These pine nuts are very similar to the European

Small chicha pitcher

A. Osorio Luque (1913-1979) "Car loaded with sugar cane", Tucumán, 1976

chestnuts and even today the Indians in the south are allowed to collect them.

With the wild strawberry, Llahueñ, (Fragaria chilensis), the Indians also prepared a drink called **Piquillín**. Auguste M. Guinnard, who lived with the Indians for three years, says: "The bush that produces this strawberry has many leaves and they are bristly with thorns, the bigger leaves and the smaller ones as well, for this reason the harvest is very difficult. The Indians use a very comfortable and easy system: they put a piece of leather under the plant and the strawberries fall on it while they hit the branches with a stick. The strawberries are put in leather saddlebags that hang from the horse and while they gallop, the strawberries are mashed into a syrup that has the colour of wine."

Pulperías

The pulpería was the store, the tavern, and the playground, all in one and in the middle of nowhere. D. F. Sarmiento, an Argentine President and writer, called it "the gaucho's club"; it was the meeting place of the peasantry and a forced stop for travellers. There they went to buy tobacco, yerba mate, sugar, soap, candles, salt, oil, fat, crackers and if the store was near the city, one could also get bread there.

At the bar, which was always protected by an iron grill, one could drink caña, *vino Carlón* (a red wine brought from Spain, made in Sanlúcar de Barrameda, in the Province of Cádiz), *sangría* (Carlón wine with water and sugar), sour orange juice (orange juice with sugar, fresh water or caña).

Juan León Pallière (1823-1887) "Pulpería"

The owners of the pulperías were almost always Catalans or Andalusians and as time passed by, Italians took over; the customers were almost exclusively men.

These stores were used as post office, bank, news agency, dance floor, sports field (they played *sortija* and *pato*), race course; here they played cards and *taba*; here they had the opportunity of meeting people, of dancing, singing, drinking, playing and quarrelling.

"Here they meet strangers and acquaintances, and imbibe *caña*. Then they indulge in cards, music, singing and dancing, and soon get excited by the strongest feeling of rivalry." *(Hinchliff)*

Old pulpería glass

Old pulpería glass

Wines

Every year in Mendoza in March the traditional Fiesta de la Vendimia (Vintage Celebration) takes place.

On his second voyage, Christopher Columbus brought vine and wheat plants to America, but neither vine nor wheat bore fruit in the Antilles.

The plants were transported on board in big barrels and were left on deck so that they could have air and light. When Hernán Cortés took vine stocks from Extremadura (Spain) to Mexico in 1520, he was luckier. In 1539 the first winery was established in America.

Then Francisco Pizarro and Diego de Almagro took stocks to Peru and from there they were taken to Chile and Argentina.

In 1566 the first vines are planted in the Province of Mendoza. This Mendoza wine was transported to Buenos Aires on mules, in a voyage that lasted for days and days and in the heat of the sun, all factors that did not necessarily improve the quality of the wine. The better wine was brought from Spain and Portugal. Many times, the wine producers from Mendoza complained about it and their case even went to the Spanish Court, but their requests were never attended to. Surely the patriots in 1810 toasted with Spanish wine. After this date and very slowly, the wine cultivated at the foot of the Andes began to be drunk in the Argentine.

E. E. Vidal (1791-1861) "Wine Mules"

When the railway line to Mendoza was inaugurated in 1885, the production was transported by train and the quality of the wine improved.

Vines grow in a semiarid fringe at the foot of the Precordillera de los Andes (foothill of the Andes), from the Province of Salta in the north down to the Province of Río Negro (Black River) and part of the Province of Chubut in Patagonia. Along this high plain (600 to 800 meters above sea level) the same vinestocks have been planted.

The hight of the plain ensures rigorous winters, which are needed for these plants. Rain in the area is very scarce, often in form of hail which can ruin an entire vineyard in a few seconds.

The plants depend totally on meltwater that is carried to the vineyards by a large system of canals. To counteract the strong sun, the plants are pruned in a way that allows the grapes to mature under a roof of leaves.

Although the Province of Mendoza produces 70% of the total production of wine in Argentina, the Provinces of San Juan, La Rioja, Salta and the Valley of the Río Negro, also have excellent wines.

The Argentine has the best red wines in South America and its Malbec is the best in the world. The Malbec variety which originated in Bordeaux is cultivated in Mendoza. Among white wines, the most famous is the aromatic Torrontés, which originated in Spain; today the Provinces of La Rioja and Salta produce an excellent Torrontés.

In the second half of the XIX th century, Italian, German, and French immigrants brought and cultivated stocks imported from Europe which improved the quality of the wine.

Lagrimilla was the first Argentine wine drunk at the court of the Spanish King. It was produced at the jesuitic farm of Jesús María, in the Province of Córdoba.

John Miers
"Wine production in Mendoza", 1826

Drinks

Sugar bowl
Colonial silver

In colonial times water was taken from house to house by the aguatero, the watercarrier who drew water from the Río de la Plata, or it was drawn from wells with beautifully ornamented iron wrought structures. Needless to say that this water was of much better quality. The other non-alcoholic drinks that were and are still drunk today, besides water and milk, are mate, coffee and chocolate.

Mate, Argentina's national drink, is drunk not only by Argentine people but many people in the rest of the world who are learning to enjoy it.

Mate is an excellent beverage. It not only stimulates the nervous system and the circulation, but it is an excellent regulator of the digestive system as well.

Yerba Mate has an important beneficial action on those portions of the brain responsible for the memory and it helps to recover from mental fatigue.

Mate from Mendoza

Carlos E. Pellegrini
(1800-1875)
"Waterman"

To have **coffee** with a friend at a bar, is an Argentine habit. The porteño (native of Buenos Aires, the port), for instance, can spend hours in front of a cup of coffee and no waiter would even dream of asking him to go, although there may be people waiting to get a free table.

Going to the "café de la esquina" (the café round the corner) is a Latin habit, the café used to be a male preserve as the pulperías had been in the country.

At the café one can order a *café* (coffee in a small cup), a *cortado* (cortado means cut, cut with some milk), a *café doble* (double coffee in a bigger cup), or a *café con leche* (coffee with a lot of milk in a big cup, generally drunk for breakfast).

Chocolate originated in Mexico, and in colonial times, chocolate was drunk in Argentina almost every day, but nowadays it is not as common as it used to be. It was prepared in big silver *chocolateras*, chocolate jars.

*Chocolate Jar
Colonial silver*

Chocolate with Milk

Ingredients
4 cups of milk
1 cup of water
1-2 bars of chocolate for each cup , sugar

Dissolve the chocolate bars in a cup of previously heated water and add sugar and milk and put it on low fire, do not let it boil because if chocolate boils, it loses its aroma.

At the *cafés* one can order a **submarino**, which is a fast way of preparing chocolate. One gets a big cup of very hot milk with a big bar of chocolate which will eventually melt in the milk. Sugar is usually added to the submarine.

Milk was brought on horseback from the small farms and estancias near the cities. "Milk is brought on horseback in earthen or tin bottles, four and sometimes six of which are carried by each horse in hide pockets, attached to the saddle, and laced up with a piece of thong." (E. E. Vidal)

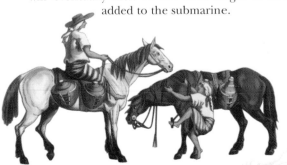

Emmeric Essex Vidal (1791-1861) "Milkmen"

Cheese

On March 9th. 1803, Juan Hipólito Vieytes publishes in his weekly *Agriculture, Industry and Trade,* a method of manufacturing good quality cheese. He even includes a recipe in his article. Until that moment, the cheese eaten in the colony was almost always brought from Europe or prepared at home with recipes brought from Spain. Vieytes, logically, advised the people who had large estancias, to produce cheese in the country. Many followed his piece of advice, and started with the production of Argentine cheese.

At the end of the XVIIIth century, small shops began manufacturing cheese; they used to sell it from house to house.

Today the dairy industry in Argentina produces excellent cheese, many of which have European denominations: Camembert, Cheddar, Fontina, Provolone, Gruyère, Reggiano, etc. All these varieties are manufactured using recipes brought from Europe. But the taste of food varies according to the place where it is produced, there are several factors that influence this difference: climate, water, soil and raw material. The taste of food does not travel well.

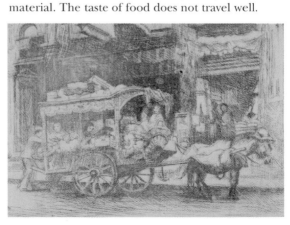

Guillermo Dohme, "Salesman", 1966

The Best Argentine Cheese

Goya: cheese of semi-tough paste, produced in the Province of Corrientes has a spicy and lightly salted flavour, it is used grated in cookery.

Chubut, Huemul and Mar del Plata: they are of semi-tough paste and very similar to Dutch cheese.

Huemul is probably the best Argentine cheese.

Tafí: tastes like Cantal, of tough paste, it matures at the foot of the Cumbres Calchaquíes in the Province of Tucumán. In Tafí they say that this cheese is made of milk flavoured with the fragrant pastures of the region.

Cheese from Tandil

Cafayate: semi- soft cheese, of very good flavour, it is manufactured in the Province of Salta.

Atuel: dessert cheese, similar to Port Salut.

Tandil: cheese of tough paste.

Salteño: cheese from the Province of Salta seasoned with pepper.

Quesillo: this goat cheese is eaten together with arrope (a very thick syrup made from the fruit of the mistol (Zisiphus mistol) or the tuna (Cactus opuntia, see page 68), of elastic paste. Its preparation starts with cheese that has been left to air for some time and which is cut into fine slices and put into boiling salt water. When the cheese begins to form fibres, it is taken out of the water and kneaded until achieving a soft and flat paste. It is then left to dry in the open air on a lattice of canes.

Provolone is usually eaten with asado. It is grilled with olive oil and sprinkled with pepper and oregano. It has to be left on the grill for a very short time because it has to be soft but it should not melt.

In Tafí del Valle, in february, the annual Cheese Fair is celebrated, where prizes for the best cheese are awarded. Some of the cheese manufactured in the valley are not drained in a mould but in a sort of basket made of straw and then pressed between two stones.

Desserts

Desserts vary according to the region in which they are prepared, only Dulce de Leche (see page 66) reigns in the whole country.

In the north, desserts with a big amount of eggs are famous: flan, ambrosia, huevos quimbos. In the south, they prepare jams made of calafate (Berberis heterophyla), rhubarb, strawberries and raspberries. In the Northwest, they make tuna and fig jam (prickly pear) and in the Northeast, mamón jam is prepared (Papaya carica communis).

Mamón or papaya (Papaya carica)

Flan

Flan (a sort of custard) is together with ice cream and postre vigilante (see page 71), the most asked for dessert at a restaurant. It is of Spanish origin, but the native flan has a difference: it is eaten topped with dulce de leche.

Ingredients
1 l milk , 3/4 cup sugar, 4 eggs, 2 yolks, vanilla essence, caramel made of 100 gr sugar and water

Boil the milk with the sugar and stir with a wooden tablespoon until the sugar is dissolved. Beat the eggs and the yolks with some drops of vanilla essence and pour the milk into this preparation, stirring constantly. Strain the preparation and put it inside a custard mold with the caramel. Put the mold inside a tin filled with water and cook it in the low oven during 1 hour. It is ready when one introduces a knife into it and it comes out clean.

Caramel
"Put 100 gr sugar in a saucepan, add a spoonful water and put it on the fire, stirring from time to time, until it is mixed and turns brown."
(Mrs. Petrona C. de Gandulfo)

Dulce de Leche

In 1908, the dairy factory La Martona, in Cañuelas, was the first establishment that manufactured dulce de leche. Today around 120.000 tons of dulce de leche are made and some 3.500 tons are exported.

Half of all Argentine desserts would disappear if dulce the leche did not exist. When abroad, Argentine people who have no dulce de leche, suffer the syndrome of abstinence and all those who go abroad, take dulce de leche in their luggage. Dulce the leche is the national obsession.

When foreigners try it for the first time, they usually think it is far too sweet, but after some time they develop the same passion.

Its origin is uncertain, but there is a legend about its origin, and as with all legends there is probably some truth in it. In the year 1829, Juan Manuel de Rosas was in Cañuelas, in the Province of Buenos Aires, when General Juan Lavalle, who was not precisely his friend, paid him a visit. Rosas was not in the camp and Lavalle, who happened to be very tired, lay down on Rosas camp bed and fell asleep.

Albérico Isola, (1817-1850) "Uses and Customs of Buenos Aires", 1844

When the servant, who was preparing the lechada, (sugar dissolved in milk for the mate) saw Rosas' enemy fast asleep in her master's bed, she immediately ran out, looking for Rosas and leaving the lechada boiling slowly on the embers. When Rosas returned, he said that Lavalle should not be disturbed, and the servant returned to the kitchen. The lechada was brown, but its taste was excellent. Dulce de leche, caramelised milk, had been invented. This happened on July 17th, 1829.

Ingredients
3 l milk
1 kg sugar dissolved in 1/2 l of hot water
1 vanilla pod
1 pinch of bicarbonate of sodium

Boil the milk with the bicarbonate (use a copper saucepan, if possible, to ensure good heat distribution) and add the sugar and vanilla. Allow the mixture to boil gently and do not stop stirring. This should be done with a long-handed wooden spoon for about 50 minutes, and one has to pay special attention for the jam not to burn or stick. The mixture should have the colour of caramel.
Once the jam is ready, stir until it cools down. To speed up the process, put the copper saucepan into another pan filled with cold water.

"As this is the fruit season, a number of people were crying peaches up and down the streets, but on horseback, with large panniers, made of the raw hides of oxen, on each side. Milk in large tin canisters, was cried about in the same way, and as they passed in a tolerable trot, I expected every moment to hear the cry changed to that of butter." (Brackenridge)

Huevos Quimbos

Apparently *huevos* (eggs) *quimbos* are a dessert of A-rab origin brought to America by the Spaniards. They are cooked in small moulds called *quimberas*.

César H. Bacle
(1794-1838)
Habits of Buenos Aires, "The Baker"

Ingredients
8 yolks, 1 egg white
1 spoonful self-rising flour, caramel

Beat the yolks and egg white until they are blended; they must have a whitish colour, sieve the flour into the mixture. Brush the quimberas with butter and put flour in them, fill them and cook them in the oven until they are golden brown, not more than 15 minutes. Turn the preparation down onto caramel. Serve cold.

Ambrosía

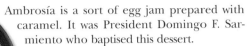

Ambrosía is a sort of egg jam prepared with caramel. It was President Domingo F. Sarmiento who baptised this dessert.

Ambrosía was in Greek mythology the food that gave the gods immortality.

Ingredients
12 yolks, 1/4 l water
1/2 kg sugar

The yolks must be beaten until they become white. With the sugar and water prepare a medium caramel and slowly pour the yolks into the caramel. Mix slowly until the yolks curdle. Serve cold.

Arrope de Tuna

Tuna (Prickly pear) (Cactus opuntia), Florian Paucke, (1719-1779)

Juan León Pallière, (1823-1887) "Baker at San Martin's Street, Buenos Aires"

In the province of Santiago del Estero, tuna (Cactus opuntia), a sort of prickly pear, grows naturally. Its fruit resembles a fig.

Ingredients
2 kg tuna, 1/2 l water

Peel the tunas, cut them into pieces and put them in a copper saucepan covered with water. Cook until the tunas are tender and mashed, and then rub it through a sieve to separate the flesh of the tunas from the seeds. Put the mixture in the saucepan again and cook until it thickens. Arrope has a very dark colour and should be like syrup. Reduce the heat to keep it just below boiling point, the soft heat of embers is perfect. Stir with a long handle wooden spoon.

Alfajores

The word *alfajor* is of Arab origin, *alfahúa* means honeycomb. In Argentina alfajores are two circular pieces of pastry stuck to each other with fig or peach jam, and more often than not, with dulce de leche. It is a sort of biscuit sandwich.

Colaciones from Córdoba

Ingredients
2 cups flour
1/2 teaspoonful baking powder, 8 yolks
1 tablespoonful sugar
1/2 glass caña or rum

Mix the ingredients, cut the round colaciones (5 cm in diameter), prick them with a fork and put them in the hot oven. Once the forms are cold, fill them with dulce de leche and cover them with icing made of sugar and hot water.

Alfajores from Santa Fé

Ingredients
600 gr flour, 1 pinch of salt
4 yolks, 200 cc water
120 gr fat

For the icing
400 gr sugar, 1 cup water, 2 egg whites

Put the flour onto the working surface and make a well in the centre. Then put the yolks, salt, water and melted fat in the centre. Knead well for some minutes and allow the mixture to rest for a while. Then knead it again. Roll out, cut the round biscuits and put them in the oven on a greased baking-sheet.

When they are cool, stick them together with jam or dulce de leche.

For the icing, prepare syrup with sugar and water. Then add the syrup to the egg whites, which have been previously whisked to froth, beating thoroughly until the icing will stand in peaks. Brush the icing on the alfajores.

Peanuts

The peanut plant (Arachis hypogaea) originated in northern Argentina and the native Indians used to eat peanuts either fried or toasted, together with corn. It is not a dry fruit, as it is usually believed, but a vegetable.

In the streets of Buenos Aires it is difficult to resist when one smells the scent of candied peanuts: this mixture of sugar and peanuts is called garrapiñada.

*Peanuts
(Arachis hypogaea),
Florian Paucke,
(1719-1779)*

Garrapiñada

*Ingredients
1 cup sugar, 1 cup water
3/4 cup raw, peeled peanuts*

Put the sugar and the water in a copper saucepan and cook them slowly until caramel is formed. Then add the peanuts and stir with a wooden spoon until the peanuts are completely caramelized.

Postre Vigilante

One of the most famous Argentine desserts is the Postre Vigilante (Policeman Dessert), Jorge Luis Borges' favourite dessert. Its preparation is extremely easy: a slice of cheese with a slice of quince preserve.

AMERICA

Calendar

Parties, festivities and celebrations are always related to food and the celebrations, especially those in places far from Buenos Aires, are a mixture of Indian, Spanish, and other European immigrants' traditions.

In the Northwest, there are many festivities that the Indians celebrated long before the Spanish conquerors arrived.

Sugar cane
(Sacharum officinarum)

In Salta, Jujuy and Catamarca, on **August 1st** the festivity of the Pachamama is celebrated. Pachamama is the Mother Earth, the goddess who protects men and animals and who makes crops grow. To pay tribute to her, a hole is made in the earth and coca, wine and desserts are put into it. One should bear in mind that almost all Indians in the North chew coca even today and coca tea can be drunk in almost all public cafeterias or hotels in Salta and Jujuy.

On August 1st, they eat bread with chicharrones, locro, empanadas, they drink chicha, wine, and they cook api, a hot mazamorra prepared with sugar, lemon and cinnamon thickened with corn flour.

On that same day, in Chaco, a province in the Northeast, early in the morning and on an empty stomach, before the first mate, people drink a mixture of ruda macho (Ruta graveolens, a small plant found in almost all gardens in Argentina, kept for luck) and caña, to protect themselves against all illnesses that August might bring.

Ruda
(Route graveolens)

They also perfume their houses with incense to protect them against evil spirits.

In Santiago del Estero on August 1st, alcuco, a thick soup made with ground wheat, charqui or goat's meat is prepared. It is believed that on that day,

Jacob van Meurs,
"Allegory of America"
Amsterdam, 1671

"Gnocchi of the 29th"
On the 29th of each
month, in Argentina
people eat gnocchi.
The habit is to put
money under the
dish. The money has
to be spent on food
the following day.

Tanico with his big hat freely roams the kitchens. Tanico is the devil become man and the word means hunger. They prepare alcuco to show that they are prosperous so that Tanico, the personification of hunger, goes away.

On **November 2nd**, Day of All Souls, in Jujuy people prepare the favourite food of the dead, this is not only a way of remembering them. In the Quebrada de Humahuaca, it is believed that on that day, the dead actually visit their houses. With bread dough, figures of small animals and angels are prepared, and they put them on a small altar and wait for the arrival of their souls.

Anonymous
"Flight to Egypt",
Cuzco, XVIII th
century

For all religious celebrations, many of the immigrants cherish their customs and traditions, but, unluckily, the native agrarian cycle does not coincide with the European cycle: in Argentina **Easter** is in autumn and **Christmas** in summer. For Christmas, in spite of the heat, the descendants of these immigrants insist on preparing pastries with nuts, almonds, and honey, rum and chocolate. The Germans prepare Stollen, the Welsh their cakes loaded with dry fruits, the Spaniards their *turrón* and the Italians make their excellent *panettone*. This sweet bread, the high one, baked in a special form that resembles the Neapolitan Sweet Bread, is the *pan dulce* baked in the Argentine.

On **January 6th**, Twelfth Night, people all over the country prepare a large ring-shaped cake. Inside this Epiphany cake, a small present is hid, usually a porcelain figure representing Baby Jesus. The person who finds it, will be lucky the whole year round. In the north, for Twelfth Night, chipás are

Anonymous
Cuzco, XVIII th century,
"Last Supper"

served. Carnival is practically not celebrated in Buenos Aires. In Corrientes or in the Provinces of the
Northwest, dancing is accompanied with a lot of
chicha, empanadas, corncobs and quesillo.

In colonial times, fast days were rigorously observed
so much so that very few animals were slaughtered:
"only for children or sick people", but as Lent is in
autumn, abstinence from meat is compensated with
the abundance of fruit.
On Good Friday empanadas made of vegetables, fish
and shellfish are prepared. For Easter Sunday a ring-
shaped cake is baked, it includes hard-boiled eggs.
For Easter, rabbits, eggs, and hens made of chocolate are also eaten, a habit brought by most of the
immigrants from Northern Europe.
For **June 24th**, day of St John, in the Provinces in the
north, enormous bonfires are lit; people celebrate
the winter solstice eating boiled matambre, chicharrones bread, chipá bejú and manioc empanadas.
On **June 29th**, Day of St Peter and St Paul, all along
the Atlantic coast, fishermen celebrate their Patron
St Peter, preparing hake with cider.

*"Chocolate and sweet
cakes is the common
breakfast of the higher
orders, soup having a
hodge-podge of pork
cut small, beef, pease,
and numerous veg-
etables; or another
sort with eggs, bread,
and spinnage with
meat in tatters is the
first course; which is
followed by beef, roast-
ed to rags, and final-
ly by fish...The ladies
drink nothing but wa-
ter, and the gentlemen
regale either on white
wine of St. Juan or the
red from Mendoza..."*
(A. Gillespie, 1818)

Weights and Measures

The units of measurement used in Argentine recipes are kilograms, grams and litres or, to make things easier, the contents of cups, tablespoons, etc.

In old recipes, the quantities were never clearly indicated, except for, surprisingly, the quantity of eggs, which was always specified. The other ingredients were named vaguely: "a pinch of sugar", "a lot of flour", and "a handful of parsley".

Albérico Isola, "Habits and Customs in Buenos Aires", 1844

Liquid			Solid	
150 ml	1/4 pint	2/3 cup	25 gr	1 oz
300 ml	1/2 pint	1 1/4 cups	100 gr	4 oz
450 ml	3/4 pint	2 cups	350 gr	12 oz
600 ml	1 pint	2 1/2 cups	450 gr	1 lb
1 litre	1 3/4 pints	41/4 cups	1 kg	2 1/4 lb

C. E. Pellegrini (1800-1875) "Hut", 1841

Equivalents						
1 glass	=	2 to 2.5 dl	=	7-8 fl oz	=	1 cup
5 spoonfuls	=	1 dl	=	4 fl oz	=	1/2 cup

Bibliography

H. M. Brackenridge, *Voyage to Buenos Aires*, London, 1820
Gerald Durrell, *The Whispering Land*, London, 1961
Amedée Frézier, *Chronicle*, Amsterdam, 1717
A. Gillespie, *Gleanings and Remarks*, Leeds, 1818
J. M. Gorriti, *The Eclectic Kitchen*, Buenos Aires, 1999
A. Guinnard, *Three Years of Captivity*, Buenos Aires, 1999
T. W. Hinchliff, *South American Sketches*, London, 1863
B. Koessler-Ilg, *Araucanos' tales*, Buenos Aires, 1996
J. Miers, *Travels in Chile and La Plata*, London, 1826
Florian Paucke, *To and fro*, Tucumán, Buenos Aires, 1943
L. V. Mansilla, *A Trip to the Ranqueles*, Buenos Aires, 1940
J. Sánchez Labrador, *Natural Paraguay*, Tucumán, 1948
U. Schmidel, *Vera Storia*, Nürnberg, 1599
E. E. Vidal, *Picturesque Illustrations*, Buenos Aires, 1943

Index

Index

Albérico Isola, "Habits and Customs in Buenos Aires", 1844